NIGHT STICK

by
JOSEPH C. HESS
Chief Instructor
Broward County Police Academy

Editor: Gregory Lee
Graphic Designer: Karen Massad

Printed in the United States of America
Library of Congress Catalog Card Number: 82-61732
ISBN: 0-89750-082-2

Second Printing 1983

OHARA PUBLICATIONS, INCORPORATED
BURBANK, CALIFORNIA

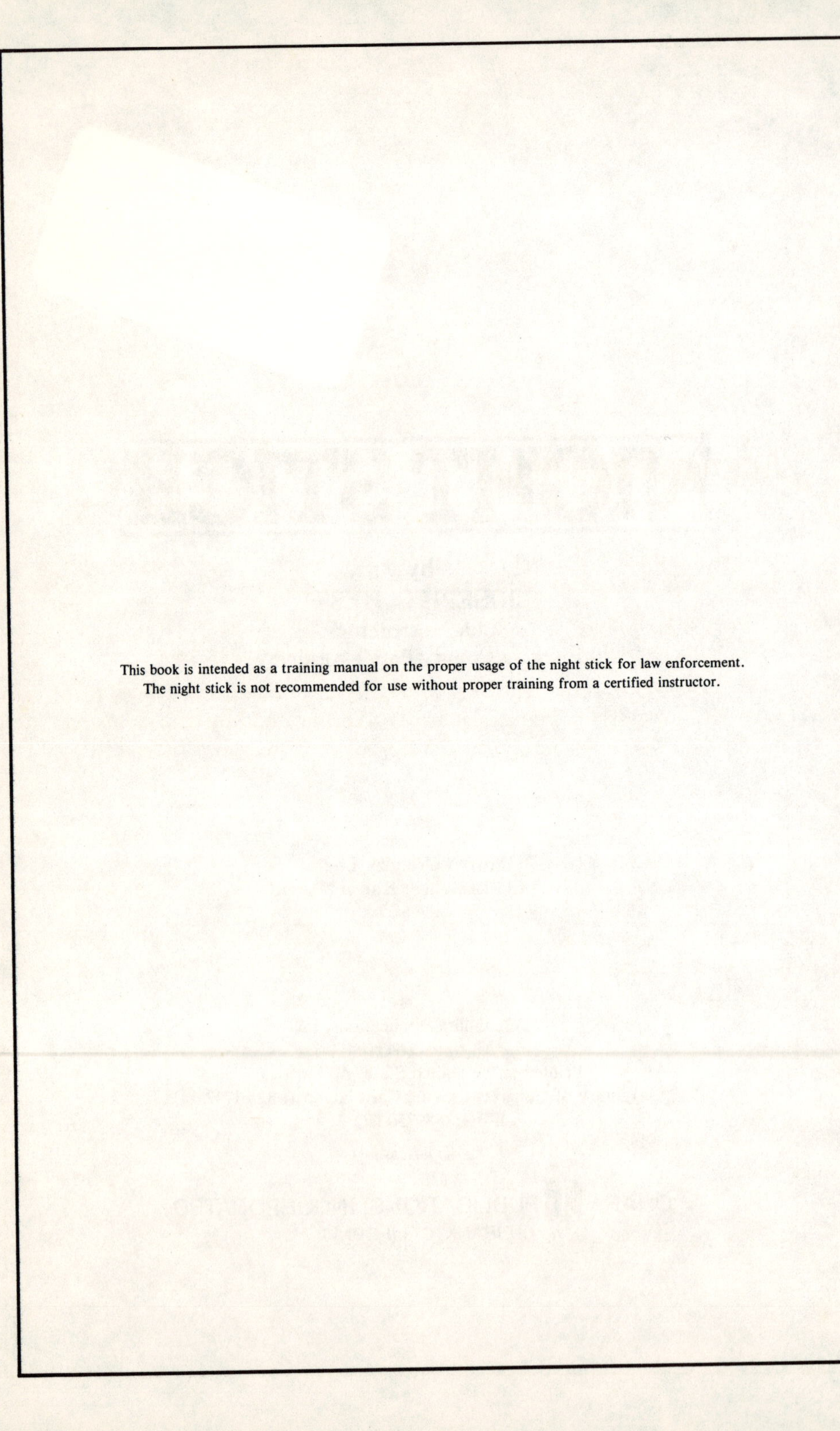

This book is intended as a training manual on the proper usage of the night stick for law enforcement. The night stick is not recommended for use without proper training from a certified instructor.

Acknowledgements

Special thanks to my two black belts who have helped me throughout the entire production of this book:

Joseph Kelljchian	Fourth degree black belt
Ronald Russell	Fourth degree black belt

Without their untiring effort and diligence, this book would not have been possible. Many hours of planning, adding and deleting have made this a working text for the law enforcement officer.

About the Author

Joseph Hess is considered one of the finest martial arts and police-training instructors in the country. He has personally been responsible for 17 black belt instructors who are currently teaching all over the country. He holds a tenth degree black belt in goju-ryu karate, a fourth degree black belt in Okinawan karate, and a red sash in the northern system of gung fu. He also holds rankings in judo, aikijitsu and jujitsu.

Hess was the world-heavyweight champion in full-contact karate from 1975-77. As a result, he has been featured in over 60 different magazine and newspaper articles, and has appeared on many local, national and international television programs, including ABC's *Wide World of Sports.* In addition, he is the author of numerous articles on physical fitness for police officers, and has written three books dealing with defensive tactics and stick fighting.

Hess is currently the chief instructor in physical training and unarmed defense for the Broward County Police Academy in Florida where he has been teaching for the past eight years. He has also traveled to South and Central America where he has trained law enforcement agencies throughout Ecuador and Mexico. A specialist in 16 different weapons, Hess teaches classes for black belts only in the use of these weapons.

Introduction

Night Stick was written to provide police officers and all law enforcement personnel with a well-rounded training program in the use of the night stick. It is extremely important to follow the guidelines in this book very carefully so that you will develop a complete, workable system under stressful situations without resorting to "deadly force."

The first portion of any training program must deal with the individual's awareness and attitudes—what his goals are and what he wants to achieve from this or any training program. Personal discipline and the desire to learn are essential. This book is designed to give you a thorough concept of what effective night stick techniques should look like, and how these techniques should be executed. As you progress with your training, however, you will have questions regarding balance, speed and control with the night stick, and these must necessarily be answered by someone who has direct personal experience with night stick use on the street and in its instruction.

Remember, during your training and throughout your career you will be called upon to deal with potentially violent situations. A majority of them do not require the use of deadly force. A nonlethal, controlled action will usually divert any attack, and you will sleep a lot better knowing that you subdued rather than killed an attacker in a situation that was manageable.

Keep in mind that the night stick is an extension of your arm. *It is not a bludgeon.* Blows to the head should be avoided at all times. A police officer is never justified in using unnecessary force.

Another important aspect of law enforcement training is physical fitness. This is one area that cannot be neglected by the police officer. I find that in the field many officers, once released from a training academy, do little or no exercise pertaining to their line of work. If you are not physically fit you cannot function to your maximum potential, especially if you are overweight. You cannot change your basic constitution, but you can minimize undesirable physical conditions by following a personal fitness program to improve your coordination, endurance, equilibrium, strength and speed. Regular and demanding physical activity not only helps your body; it can improve your personality, provide some insight into better ways of living, and help you perform your duties to the best of your ability.

During my years as a law enforcement officer I have gained a much greater understanding of people. I have found that, unfortunately, not everyone is law abiding, and that many that you come in contact with do not respect police officers. But I am glad that I have had the opportunity to serve both as a police officer and as an instructor in the martial arts. This combination has given me a well-rounded perspective on life.

My training has taken me all over the world. To date, I have trained more than 300 law enforcement agencies in the U.S. and in other countries, so I have been privileged to compare law enforcement in these countries with our system here in the U.S.

A police officer does not have an easy job out there in the street. You have to be on your toes 150 percent of the time. You must be prepared to expect the unexpected at all times. It is not always fair out there in the real world, and it is safe to assume if a suspect has the opportunity to cause you bodily harm, he will. Working constantly with the criminal element can also produce in the police officer a lax attitude toward his duty and a tendency to become fixed in his routine. An officer should never get caught in this dilemma (at worst, it could be fatal). The police officer who doesn't go with the flow, who treats every situation and person the same, will wind up getting hurt. Before he acts, the officer should try to assess every instance individually.

As someone has said, "There is no absolute answer to crime, just good police work."

—Joseph C. Hess
Fort Lauderdale, Florida
1982

The short and long bo staves served long ago as the only method of combat available to Oriental monks. This system of stick fighting became one of the most widespread weapons systems of our time.

Origins of the Night Stick

There are many stories regarding when and where the night stick first became a tool in standard police use. One such story credits the name night stick to the "constables on patrol" or "cops" who carried these sticks after dark, using them as an extension of the arm, providing the policeman with a margin of safety and a way of moving people from one place to another. The "billy club" or night stick soon developed into an offensive and defensive system of self-protection all its own. Of all modern weaponry, the night stick probably is still the best overall tool for physical police work next to the service revolver.

There are, however, even older origins of stick use in combat which are most prevalent in the Oriental martial arts or fighting systems. When taught correctly, they can provide officers with the proper night stick techniques. These systems use *jo-jitsu* (a *jo* is a short stick), *bo-jitsu* (the *bo* is a long staff), *jodo* (double) sticks and *kendo* (sword) training.

Bo and jo sticks were originally used by feudal monks of the Far East who developed a technique for using them as weapons to defend their monasteries from intruders, or against robbers on the road. Today, the systems are taught in many karate schools to

In addition to the sword-like bamboo stick, the kendo system includes a complete set of protective armor, including headgear, gloves, chest, hip and groin protectors.

help students develop power, timing, reflexes and agility in their basic body movements.

Jodo sticks, being made from bamboo, are lightweight and very fast. They are used most effectively for striking and blocking. The total jodo stick system, though, utilizes a series of takedown moves, choking and entrapment holds, and foot sweeps. Used together, they make it very difficult for an opponent to get within grabbing or striking distance. The sticks can be snapped very quickly with the proper wrist action, stunning an opponent when hit in the right area.

Kendo, or Japanese fencing, uses a sword made of bamboo, and instruction in this ancient sport can teach the law enforcement officer many good methods of blocking and striking.

The *nunchaku* was one of several weapons developed by 15th-century farmers on the island of Okinawa as a means to protect themselves from their Japanese invaders. The forerunner of the nunchaku is said to have been a farm tool used for threshing grain. The nunchaku consists of two hardwood sticks tied together with either a short rope or chain. When wielded against an attacker, it is a formidable weapon, capable of inflicting a great deal of punishment in the form of strikes, pinches and choke holds.

Many other farm implements were adapted by the clever Okinawans for use as weapons: a millstone handle became the *tonfa*, an extremely versatile club; a plow blade became the *kama*, a deadly sickle.

After World War II, American servicemen stationed in Japan realized that the nunchaku was an excellent weapon for self-protection. A complete offensive and defensive system was eventually devised for it. In police work today, the nunchaku (or "chucks") can be most effective as a "come-along" tool.

Today, the night stick is as much a part of an officer's uniform as his hat or his handcuffs. Most police departments throughout the United States generally have the same rules and characteristics governing the shape and dimensions of the patrolman's night stick. Though many new tools are constantly being developed for law enforcement work (such as the taser and nunchaku), there will always be a valuable place for the night stick.

U.S.A.

Contents

Ready Positions and Practice Exercises

It is important to learn proper use of the night stick *with both hands.* Remember: when you are striking or blocking with the stick, you are tying up the use of one hand, if not both. Keep your other hand close to your body so your opponent does not deliver a punch or kick to a vulnerable spot, or worse, reach for your service revolver.

Make sure that all your stick moves are done with a quick snap and recovery motion—*never* leave the stick out within easy reach so that it can be grabbed or taken away from you.

The following positions and simple exercises will help you gain strength and let you execute the maneuvers in the chapters that follow. It is important to keep in mind that none of these stances are static, so you should be in motion constantly, not maintaining any one position for too long.

Before starting with the ready positions, let's look closer at the body of the night stick and a commonly used optional feature, the thong.

ANATOMY OF THE NIGHT STICK

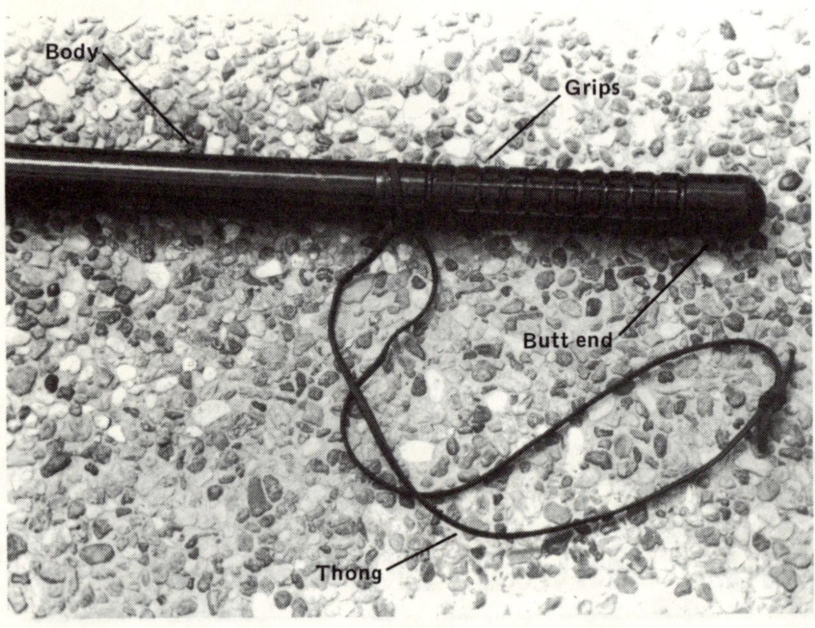

- The night stick should be made from a hardwood such as oak, ash, hickory, rock maple, or from a heavy plastic.
- The night stick should weigh not less than 15 ounces and not more than 18 ounces.
- The standard length should be about 26 inches long. Riot sticks are generally longer at around 31 inches.
- The stick shape is cylindrical with round edges, and not more than one-and-a-half inches in diameter.
- Lead or other weighted materials should not be added to the night stick.

THE THONG

The thong, a leather strap secured to the stick at the base of the grips, is used to help an officer maintain his grasp on the stick. There are, however, many police departments who do not advocate the use of the thong. Many injuries can and have occurred when a suspect grabs the night stick while the thong is wrapped incorrectly about the officer's hand.

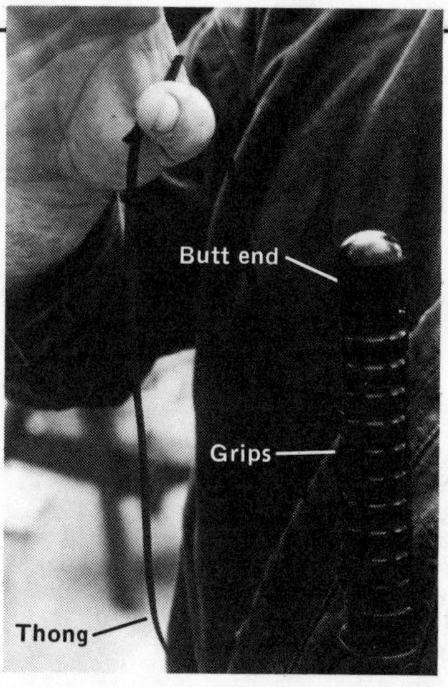

When using the thong, only your thumb should be slipped inside the thong, **not** your entire wrist.

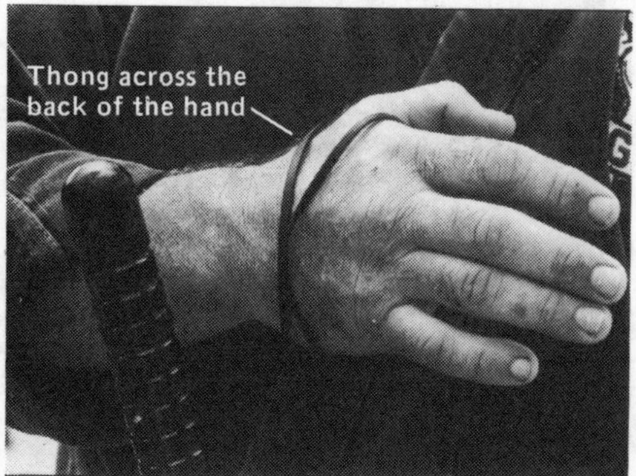

After you have placed the thong over your thumb, roll your hand over, making sure that the thong goes across the back of the hand and the night stick grips fit firmly into the palm of your hand.

If you find that the thong is too large for your hand, turn the night stick in the palm of your hand so that the thong will become snug across the back of your hand.

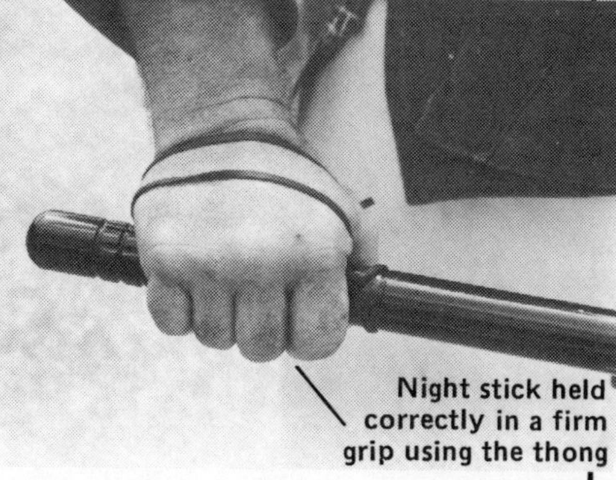

Your thumb is the key to locking the thong around your hand so that it does not bind you up if a suspect makes a grasp for your stick. The thumb enables the thong to release itself and the stick from your hand.

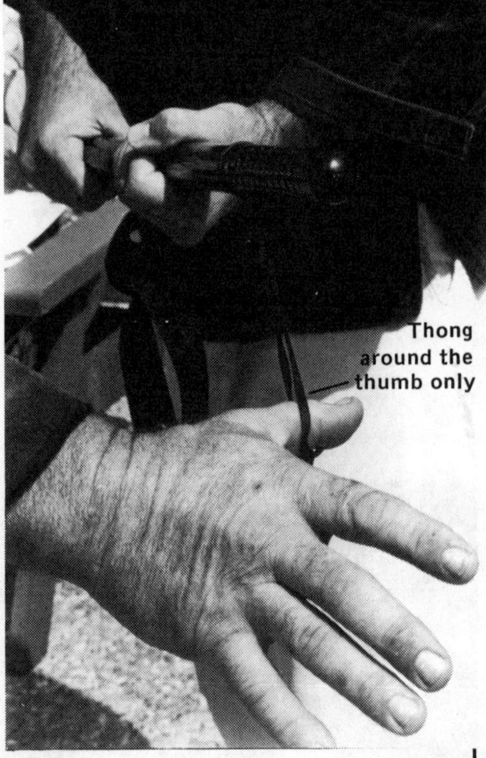
Thong around the thumb only

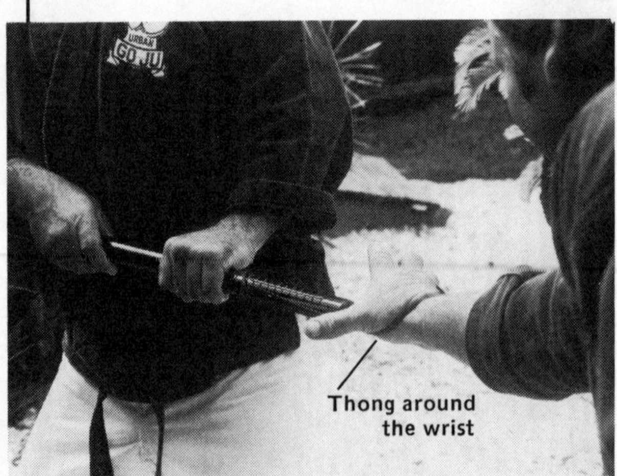

Thong around the wrist

If the thong is wrapped about your wrist, however, there is a great risk of being pulled off balance or being kicked in a vital area, because you cannot pull free fast enough.

RESTRAINING

The thong can be used effectively in an emergency as a substitute for handcuffs. By using the night stick thong, you leave one of your hands free. (1) Shows the placement of the thong on the wrist, keeping the stick near the shoulder while placing the thong around the wrist and maintaining an upward pull on the grip end. Bring the other hand of the suspect inside the thong (2) and maintain a constant upward pull on the stick to keep his wrists in check. Keep the stick tilted at an angle in case the suspect tries to pull forward so you will be able to push him to the ground. The stick should be placed flush against his back (3) with the thong wrapped tightly by rolling the stick closer to the wrists (be careful not to maintain this too long or too tightly or you will cut off the circulation in his wrists). Push him forward with the stick against his back and keep pulling the grip up to maintain control. Your free hand can now be placed on the suspect's shoulder or upper arm.

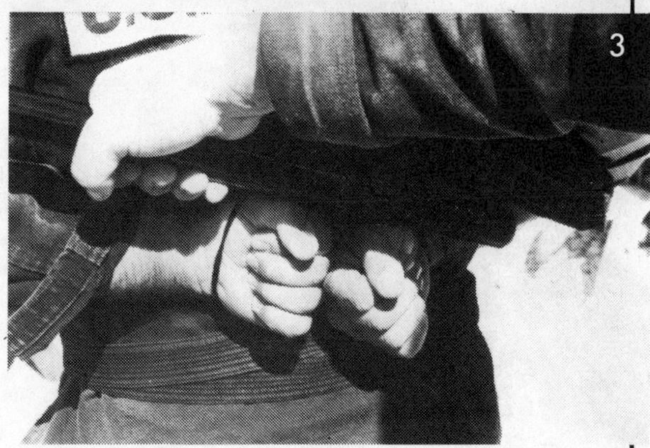

FRONT READY POSITIONS

POSITION ONE

Holding the night stick across your chest at a 45-degree angle, position your left hand at the top, with your palm facing inward toward your body, leaving about one inch of the stick exposed (which makes it difficult for an opponent to grab the stick from you). Your right hand should be held with your palm facing inward, leaving about one inch of the stick exposed at the bottom.

POSITION TWO

Move the stick away from your body either to block or strike with the end. A strike from this position would be a short snap motion, and then the stick returned to the crossed-chest position. Make sure you use a rolling motion of the wrists to give you more snap.

POSITION THREE

The night stick is held in a horizontal position, and both hands must face downward toward the ground. From here, a sharp snap motion delivers a groin block or middle-body block downward toward the opponent attacking you.

POSITIONS FOUR AND FIVE

In (4) the night stick is held away from the body at a 45-degree angle. Your left hand is placed at the top on the left side of the stick, while your right hand is at the bottom on the right side. In (5) both hands are on the same side of the stick with the right hand at the top and the left hand at the bottom. Either position is acceptable.

POSITION SIX

The night stick has been snapped into the palm of your left hand and a front ready position has been assumed. If an opponent is to be struck, the blow may be delivered with the front portion of the night stick into the solar plexus, or the main body of the stick may be used to block the groin area. All techniques like these must be executed with a snap.

POSITION SEVEN

This crossed-arm position allows you to stand ready, yet not betray to an opponent any defensive method, for it allows you the flexibility to strike to either the front or the side easily (see inset A). The crossed-arm position appears relaxed and calm, but you are ready to snap out instantly without being limited to any one particular block or strike.

REAR READY POSITIONS

POSITION ONE

This is called the horizontal relaxed ready position. It places the night stick out of view from an opponent. It can be placed into a full combat ready position with either hand with just a quick snap motion. Notice that both palms face to the rear with the stick held close to the buttocks. This stance is not used as often as a front ready position, but it does have a place in night stick work. Remember that the stick does not have any limitations from this position. You are still able to strike and, if necessary, you still have your gun hand free if the situation arises.

POSITION TWO

When you come upon an opponent whom you feel might give you some trouble, you may use this alternate method of holding the night stick to the rear. When you draw your stick from the ring, place it in your non-gun hand with the stick placed just to the rear of your shoulder. Notice that the stick stays close to the tricep or against the side of the elbow. The forefinger of the right hand is placed on the tip of the stick, and the fingers are wrapped around the night stick. If your opponent tries to grab at you or punches at you just execute a quick snap motion from behind your back (see inset A) and you will be able to block and ward off his attack. Notice that your finger is still behind the stick or just near the front end of the stick. When the block is delivered the night stick will ride the underside of your forearm.

PRACTICE EXERCISES

EXERCISE ONE

Assume a well-balanced stance, holding the night stick as shown in position six. Use force against force by pulling the front end of the stick away from the butt end for at least ten seconds. This isometric exercise will help arm strength and shoulder development. It is also very good for the fingers and wrists. As a variation, push the top hand downward while pushing the bottom hand upward, producing as much resistance as possible.

EXERCISE TWO

Assume a well-balanced stance and place the night stick in front of your chest with your palms facing down. Roll your wrists forward and backward, keeping the night stick in the same position on a horizontal plane. This is excellent for the fingers and wrists. It teaches you to keep the night stick on an even level. Try pulling both hands in opposite directions, then reverse the motion and push inward, thumb toward thumb, for at least ten seconds. Repeat each exercise at least five times.

1

2

3

EXERCISE THREE

From a ready position, step forward sharply with your right leg (1) and deliver a strike toward the ground. Stop the strike four to six inches from the ground, and keep your opposite hand held in front of your body to act as a guard. Next (2) use the guard hand to push the front of the stick toward your target area, and withdraw your right hand toward the butt end of the stick. Keep a good well-balanced stance, drop your weight down into the strike, and make sure you have a firm grip on the night stick. Finally (3), take the back end of the stick in your right hand, turn your body to the right, away from a possible leg attack, and execute a block, snapping the night stick downward. Notice that the leg being attacked is raised high, and that the left hand is held high to serve as a guard hand and to maintain balance. This should be practiced to both sides. Start out with a slow motion and work up to full speed.

1

EXERCISE FOUR

From a ready position, block across your body to the right (1) with your right hand up and your left hand down. Then block to the left (2) with your left hand up and your right hand down. Finally (3) block to the right again, this time keeping your left hand up and your right hand down. The advantage of this position is that when you block this way, the top arm can protect your face, and it allows you to deliver a strong upward blow.

Note: In each position, use isometric tension, first pushing your hands inward for a ten-second count and then pulling them outward for a ten-second count. This is excellent for developing the shoulders, wrists and fingers.

2

3

EXERCISE FIVE

From a ready position, step back (1) with your right foot, raise the night stick over your right shoulder and move your left hand into a low blocking position. Then (2) turn your body to the left, bring your right shoulder forward, and move the night stick across your body and upward. Your left hand should move upward to guard your head. Finally, (3) while turning your body to the left, bring your right foot forward and jab the night stick into your opponent's groin or stomach area. Make sure that your left hand still blocks your head, and keep your feet flat on the ground with your legs slightly bent.

Note: After practicing this drill in slow motion several times, go over it at full speed. It should take no longer than three seconds.

EXERCISE SIX

Using a partner (1), grasp each other's night stick. Then, keeping your feet flat on the floor, (2) twist back and forth, turning at the waist. Each of you must provide resistance when pushing and pulling. As you progress with this exercise, start to pick up speed and power in your thrusting motion. Doing this for at least five minutes before each training session will help establish a strong wrist and upper-body motion, and it will strengthen the lower back.

EXERCISE SEVEN

Working with a partner, start this exercise with one person holding the night stick in a vertical position (1) with both hands and arms locked. The other person then places the back of his wrist against the night stick and applies pressure against it for a count of ten seconds. (2) Then switch hands. This will help both partners develop strong wrists and shoulders.

EXERCISE EIGHT

Working with a partner (1), have one person hold the night stick high over his head in a horizontal position. The other person places his palm underneath and pushes upward for ten seconds. (2) Now reverse the action and push down on the stick held in a low horizontal position. Keep your feet flat on the floor.

Stances and Balance

Balance is achieved by the proper stance a person assumes in a given situation. Without stability, techniques are ineffective, and they place a person in jeopardy. If you have a good stance you can move rapidly and smoothly, enabling you to use the night stick more effectively. Both your body and your mind must be flexible and trained to adapt your physical and mental stances to different situations.

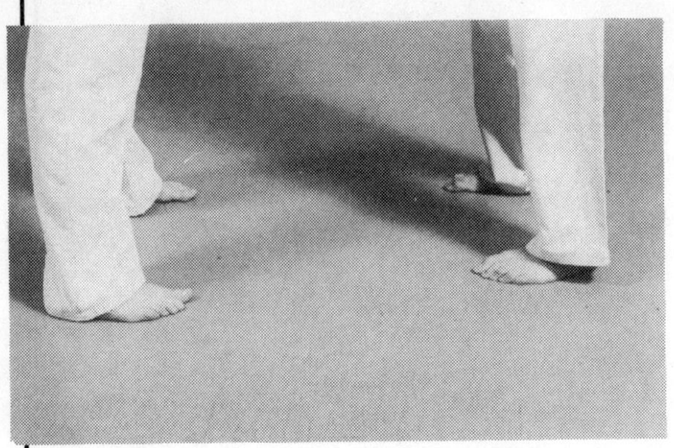

PARALLEL STANCE

The parallel stance is mostly for interrogation purposes. You must remember that if an attack seems imminent, you should adjust yourself into a more suited defensive stance. If you have a good stance you will be able to move rapidly, smoothly and effectively enabling you to effect an arrest without any problems. But you must be flexible and learn to adapt your stance to meet different situations.

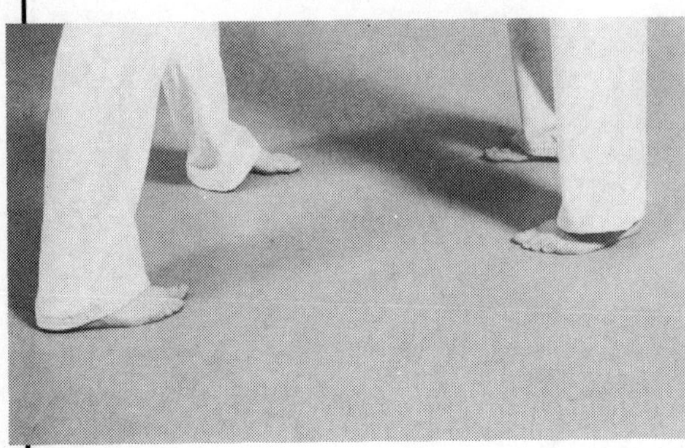

SHORT FORWARD STANCE

This short forward stance gives you a great deal of flexibility. From this stance you are able to move in any direction, and you are free to execute a kick if needed. The feet have good contact with the ground surface, and the knees are slightly bent. Your weight should be about 60 percent on the back leg.

WIDE FORWARD STANCE

This wide stance is excellent for stepping back or forward into. It gives you a great deal of power in your strikes, and It helps you distribute your weight, which should be 50 percent on each foot. Your feet should be a little wider apart than your shoulders. Your front leg should be bent, and your rear leg should be locked with your hips straight.

HALF SIDE STANCE

This stance is probably the best of all stances because when you turn half side to your opponent, you are not offering him a chance to grab for your gun. Notice that your feet are pointing at 45-degree angles to the opponent with the knees slightly bent and weight distributed evenly on both feet. This stance is also excellent for delivering a side kick if needed.

FULL SIDE STANCE

This is an excellent stance for meeting a hard attack from the front. It gives you a great deal of power in the hips and transfers the power into the strike. By standing this wide with your weight evenly distributed you are creating a distance between you and your attacker.

STRONG STANCE POSITION

To find your balance point, have a partner push your right shoulder from behind after you have placed your feet into a front forward stance. The power in your forward stance will not allow your partner to push you off balance if you are locked in. Notice that his force toward your left side has been offset by your front left leg.

WEAK STANCE POSITION

Let your partner try the same thing from the left side. Do not change the position of your feet. Notice that he will be able to easily push you off balance. The reason is that your legs are strong to either side, but if you are pushed from the center, you can be upset with no problem at all because you have nothing to back you up.

STRONG STANCE

Now have your partner push you from the front left side. If you are standing properly, when he pushes you, he will not be able to upset your balance, because you will be very strong off the right rear leg.

WEAK STANCE

Have your partner push you from the center of your body toward the rear. Notice that he will be able to upset your balance because your back leg is not in the proper position. A key point to remember here is to roll with the punches.

BALANCE EXERCISE ONE

This is a good exercise for learning and maintaining balance. Reach down and grab one ankle with both hands, then try to lift your leg up and hold it straight out in front of your body, at least waist height, for about five seconds. Learn to put all of your weight on your support foot. This is especially good for the legs and the lower back.

BALANCE EXERCISE TWO

Reach down and grab the outside part of your right foot with your right hand. Try to lift your leg up over the top of your shoulder. At the same time bring your left hand up and try to hold this position without falling for a five count. This will help to build your arms, shoulders and legs at the same time.

BALANCE EXERCISE THREE

Fold your arms in front of your body. Bring your left leg up and against your right leg with light pressure. Your right leg should be bent. Shut your eyes and try to hold that position without falling for a 15 count. If you have trouble with this, bend your support leg a little more to lower your balance.

Striking Areas

The first section of this chapter pinpoints areas of the body that you may strike with the night stick to stop an assailant effectively and quickly without causing the person irreparable harm. Any strike with the night stick is only to be used when an attack is imminent. These strikes illustrated here are practical and will work for you when the need arises. If you stick to these strikes, you should be able to control any situation.

The second section of this chapter, "Danger Zones," illustrates areas of the body that you should never strike with the night stick. *You are never justified in using unnecessary force.* Remember that whatever you are carrying in your hand is just an extension of you. *You are the weapon.* If you must raise your night stick above your own head to hit an attacker, *stay away from his head.* Strike the collarbone, the shoulder, or possibly the side of the neck.

You never know how hard to strike someone until you actually deliver the first blow. If that blow is too weak, your attacker may win out. If the blow is too hard you may cause severe damage. The only way to improve your reactions is to practice with the night stick and know the limitations of the night stick. This is the key to any training method—knowing your own power and limitations.

EFFECTIVE STRIKING AREAS

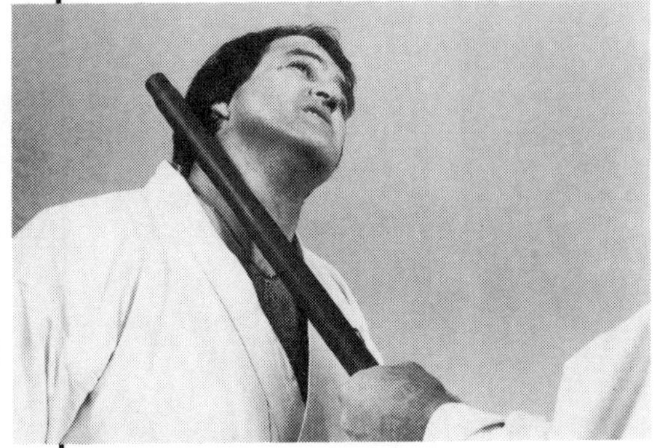

SIDE OF THE NECK

If you must strike the neck for any reason, try to strike the side. **Stay away from the windpipe area.** Try to strike the neck just where it connects with the shoulder. Do not strike with the intention of breaking the neck. A short snap motion is all that is needed.

COLLARBONE

When you really need the stopping power, this strike will disable your opponent. When you use this strike, strike directly into the clavicle, or collarbone. The many nerve endings located here cause a great deal of pain, and if the proper force is employed you can actually break the collarbone. Use this strike only if the situation warrants this type of force.

GROIN OR STOMACH

Thrust or poke strikes are excellent if they are directed toward an opponent's lower stomach area or groin. Make sure when you strike these areas that you drop your weight and drive your shoulders into the delivery. A sharp snap may be employed after you use this method.

SOLAR PLEXUS

A fast way to stop anyone from grabbing you is to strike the solar plexus with a good forward thrust upward, because there is no protection for this area. A full powered-thrust, however, could cause heart and lung damage, and possibly break the sternum. If you use this strike, remember to snap the front end of the night stick sharply with a recoil motion. Don't leave it out to be grabbed by your attacker. Since most people when struck in this area fall forward and double over, step back out of their reach and stay alert for a counterattack.

LEG

If you have your opponent down and his legs come up, strike the highest point first. This will stop any type of sweep or takedown attempt.

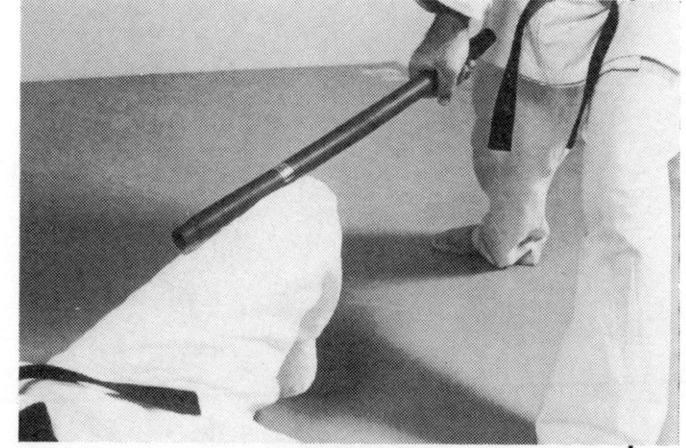

KNEE

Usually a good sharp strike to the kneecap or to the side of the knee will effectively stop an opponent. A good snapping motion should be employed when striking here.

BACK OF KNEE

A sharp blow to the rear of the knee will cause your opponent to lose his balance completely. This is also good if you find that he tries to run from you. With a short twisting motion of the night stick, rolling it counterclockwise, you can add more snap to the strike.

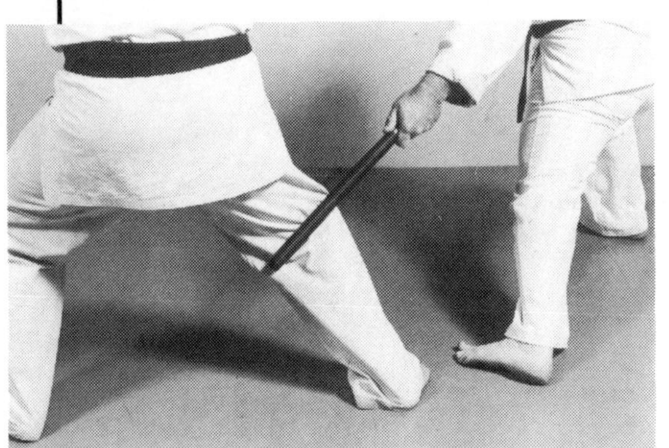

BACK OF LEG

If you miss hitting directly behind the knee, strike the upper leg. Hitting this area will cause a stinging effect on the muscle of the upper leg. You have the option of also dropping down and striking the calf muscle of the lower leg, or the heel may be a good target for you at this point.

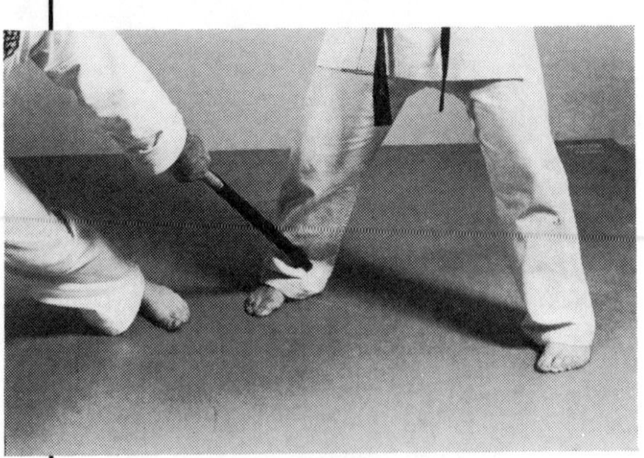

SHIN

Any direct force to the shinbone can cause severe pain. And with just a slight turn of the stick, you may also strike the anklebone. Use a snap motion and move in a circular motion away from your opponent. Remember to keep your body weight low and have a well-balanced stance at all times.

GROIN

With a slight twisting motion of your body, you can execute a snap strike to the groin. This is a very good maneuver for stopping a big man. Use a good snap motion and deliver the technique straight up.

ARMPIT

A sharp blow may be driven up into the armpit area. It contains very sensitive nerve endings which when struck cause severe pain, thus immobilizing your opponent. But be careful not to let your opponent trap the night stick under his arm.

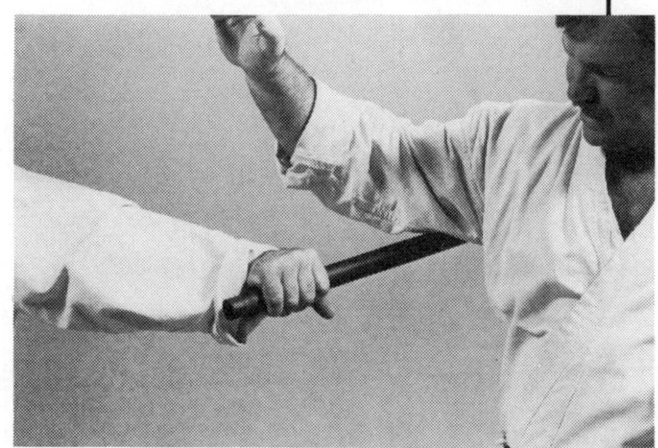

THE WRIST

A strike to the inside of the wrist is executed when you have no room to jump out of your opponent's attack. When striking, try to hit the forearm or thumb. A sharp blow to the outside of the wrist (see inset A) is also very effective.

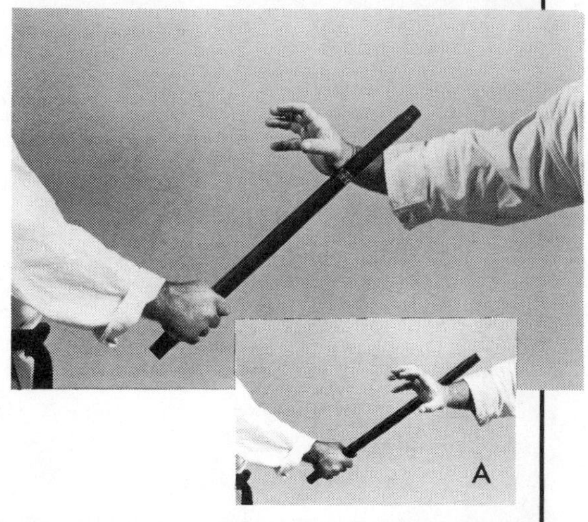

DANGER ZONES

The following are areas of the body that you should never attempt to strike with the night stick. There are too many other ways of controlling or stopping an attacker without delivering a potentially fatal blow to the head or throat. To repeat, you are never justified in using unnecessary force.

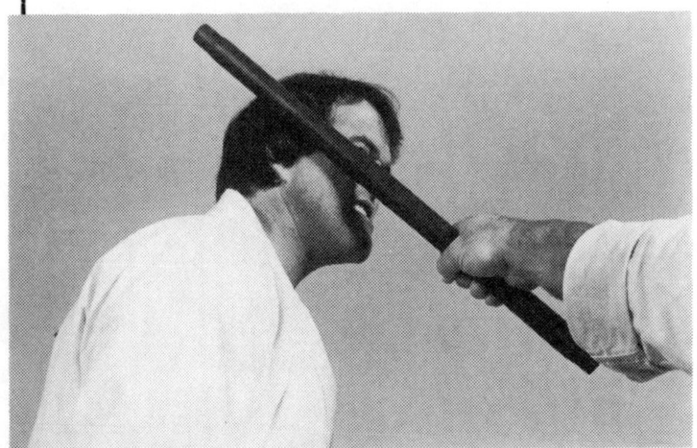

TEMPLE

Delivering a blow to the temple could cause severe brain damage or instant death. **Do not strike this area.**

BACK OF HEAD

This area of the head is known as the occipital region. A blow to this area could cause permanent damage to the eyes or to the spine. **Do not strike this area.**

BACK OF NECK

This area could also cause severe damage, mainly to the lower portion of the neck. A lower blow could cause spinal damage or a loss of hearing. **Do not strike this area.**

UPPER LIP

A blow to the upper lip is not recommended as it could drive the cartilage of the nose up into the brain, which could cause death. This type of blow could also break all the teeth in the front of the mouth. **Do not strike this area.**

BRIDGE OF NOSE

Just as serious is a blow delivered to the bridge of the nose. A strong blow could cause the loss of sight, a skull fracture, or it could snap the base of the neck. **Do not strike this area.**

FRONT OF NECK

Striking the Adam's apple could result in a blockage of air, possibly causing death. It does not take much force to injure someone when striking them with a direct blow to the throat. Severe damage to the windpipe may result. **Do not strike this area.**

HEAD

Never strike an opponent to the head area when he has been knocked down. Instead, strike other bone areas.

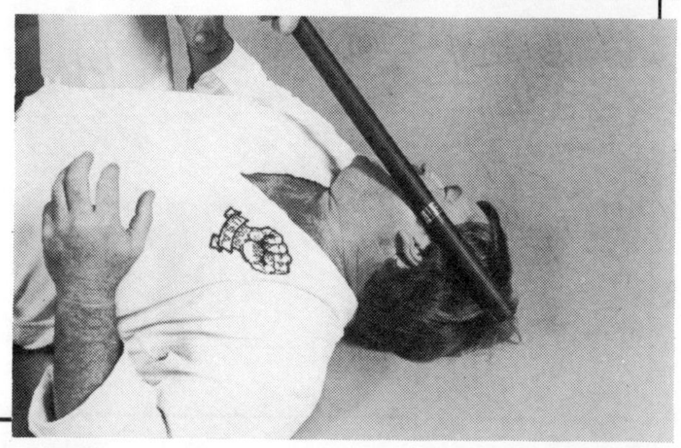

Blocking Techniques

Executing an effective block is just as important as executing an effective strike. It is the block that often opens up an opportunity for you to execute a strike. But if the block is weak, the opportunity will never arise.

Never block with a flatfooted stance. Always remain in motion. When you do execute a block, try to do it on an angle so you can deflect the attack weapon rather than just stopping it. That will open up the possibility of a strike for you.

Always remember that if the attack comes in at you vertically (as with an overhead attack), you should block horizontally. Conversely, if the attack comes in horizontally from the side, your block should be vertical.

SIDE BLOCK

When an attack comes in from the side, your stick should be raised vertically away from your body. In order to achieve maximum blocking power, drive your top hand (in this case the right hand) upward as you block.

OVERHEAD BLOCK

When blocking an overhead attack, always step back first. Never step into the block. Make sure that once you have successfully blocked the attack, shift your stick either left or right on an angle so that the force of the blow deflects in that direction.

GROIN BLOCK

Should your attacker drop down to strike your groin, snap block on an angle at least 12-18 inches away from your body in a downward motion and to the left or right. Then move in quickly with a strike.

DOWNWARD GROIN BLOCK

When you use the straight downward block from the same position, drop both your shoulders and snap your opponent's weapon with a quick body drop motion. Center your weight and be ready to release either hand to execute a follow-up strike.

ONE-HAND GROIN BLOCK

The one-hand block may be done when your attacker turns away from you and tries to deliver a blow to your groin. This leaves your other hand free to counter. This block is done with the front end of the night stick using a snapping motion.

REAR OVERHEAD BLOCK

If an attacker tries to strike you from the rear, step forward and raise the night stick over your shoulder. Make sure you look over your shoulder at your opponent and angle your night stick. Once you have deflected your opponent's attack, drop down on one knee, swing around (see inset A) and strike him in the back of the knee.

Carrying and Drawing the Night Stick

In many situations it will be necessary to draw the night stick from the holding ring in a split second. Many of the attacks on you will be total surprises. You must always be ready for these attacks, and you must be able to reach, draw and overcome your attacker. The holding ring has a tendency to limit your techniques, but there are many ring techniques that are very effective.

Many of the techniques here are designed for use when you are in a confined area and have limited maneuverability. Practice each technique by alternating the feet and step both forward and back into some of the stances you've learned to deliver the strike. Remember to always maintain eye contact with your opponent (by looking over your shoulder if you are approached from the rear) and always prepare to follow up with a secondary strike if your attacker doesn't stop right away.

A belt is used in place of the ring in all pictures in this book, but all the same principles apply.

ONE-HAND DRAW

(1) When your attacker steps into your zone, quickly step back (draw-hand side), grasp the end of the night stick and (2) deliver a sharp blow to the midsection. Keep the night stick in the ring as you deliver the strike. Follow that (3&4) by drawing the stick back and (5&6) delivering a blow to the legs. Notice that the hand position does not change. The palm remains down. Then (7-10) deliver a blow to the rib cage. A full-speed snap motion is the key factor when delivering these strikes. Finally (11& 12) deliver a blow to the side of the neck or the tip of the shoulder. **Stay away from the head.**

2
3
5
6
8
9
11
12

CROSSOVER DRAW WITH OPPOSITE HAND

As your attacker (1) steps into your zone, reach (2) across your body with your opposite hand, grasp the stick, bringing the left hand up for added power and (3)

delivering a sharp blow to his midsection. Then (4&5) bring the stick back to the cocked position and (6) deliver a cross blow to his neck.

1

2

3

TWO-HAND RING TECHNIQUE

(1) If your attacker steps in too close to allow you to remove the stick to get enough power into the strike with one hand, draw the stick (2) with your opposite hand on top, or out in front with your stick-side hand near the ring. Then (3) with both hands, deliver a short thrusting blow into his solar plexus or groin.

REAR DRAW RING TECHNIQUE

This strike allows you to keep the stick in the ring and strike your attacker with surprise. The strike must be fast and hard. (1) As your attacker moves in on you, grab (2& 3) the night stick with your nearest hand, draw it up and slightly forward while it is still in the holding ring and (4) deliver a strong blow to his midsection with a backward plunging motion.

REAR DRAW OUT OF THE RING

With this strike, the night stick is removed from the holding ring, but only just enough so that the stick clears the ring and enables you to strike to the rear. (1) As your attacker moves in, grab your stick with your left hand (2) and immediately draw it (3) from the

ring. Step back with your left foot (4) and thrust the stick into his solar plexus. A good follow-up strike to the legs or arms could be added for extra protection. Notice that the right hand covers the top of the night stick and helps plunge the stick backward.

1

KNIFE DEFENSE

If you are confronted with a knife, make sure you keep a safe distance between you and your attacker so that you will have enough room to draw your night stick. Keep the stick in front of your body and use a snapping motion when striking your attacker's wrist. (1) As your attacker approaches you with a knife, reach (2) across your chest for your stick with your right hand (your gun hand if right-handed) and (3) quickly remove it. Then (4) immediately switch hands and (5) bring the stick across in front of you, striking your attacker's hand. Finally (6&7) follow that up with a front kick to his groin. This draw will free your gun hand.

3

6

2

4

5

7

Defenses Against Grabs and Stick Attacks

With any opponent, you run the risk of having him grab you or your night stick. When this does happen, there are definite techniques to follow to regain control of the situation. If your opponent is larger than you and you don't react in a swift manner, he is liable to gain the advantage over you. The key to gaining control is balance and leverage—without these two elements you will probably end up in a push-and-shove match, with the stronger of the two winning.

This chapter is divided into two sections: what to do when an opponent grabs your limbs, clothing or your night stick. The second section deals with a situation where your night stick is taken away from you, or if your opponent has a stick weapon and you do not.

Pay special attention to the stances and footwork in this chapter. If you rely solely on your upper-body power to execute these techniques, they will not work properly.

When an opponent has grabbed you and is in a position to either punch you or kick you, you must be able to react with a controlled counter movement. These techniques will place your attacker in a position where he will be unable to cause you any further injury.

CROSS-HAND TRAP DEFENSE
(Against Lapel Grab)

As your opponent (1) moves in on you, swing your stick (2) over the top of his wrist with your right hand and (3) grab it with your left arm crossed under. Finally (4) with a quick dropping motion, lean forward and pull down on the stick. This will snap his wrist and make him release his grasp.

1

2

ONE-HAND TRAP DEFENSE
(Against Wrist Grab)

Your attacker (1) has grabbed your right wrist which is holding your night stick. In response (2) raise the stick into a vertical position and grab the raised end with your left hand. Finally (3) turn the stick counterclockwise in a downward motion, forcing your attacker to the ground.

3

1

2

HEADLOCK DEFENSE
(Against Front Tackle)

(1) As your attacker moves in toward your body, lower your night stick (2&3) forcing your right hand into his left side and holding the stick in a vertical position. Then (4&5) reach around with your left hand and grab the lowest end of

3

the stick, placing him in a headlock. Finally (6) turn the stick, sufficiently trapping your opponent around the neck. Make sure that your pressure is on the side of his neck and not on the windpipe.

1

OVERHEAD DEFENSE
(Against Front Tackle)

(1) As your attacker moves in on you, raise your stick (2) over his head and (3&4) bring it straight down with force into his back. After he has fallen to the ground (5) strike a blow to any bony area of the body, preferably the (6) collarbone or (7) the rib cage.

3

6

2

4
USAGA

5

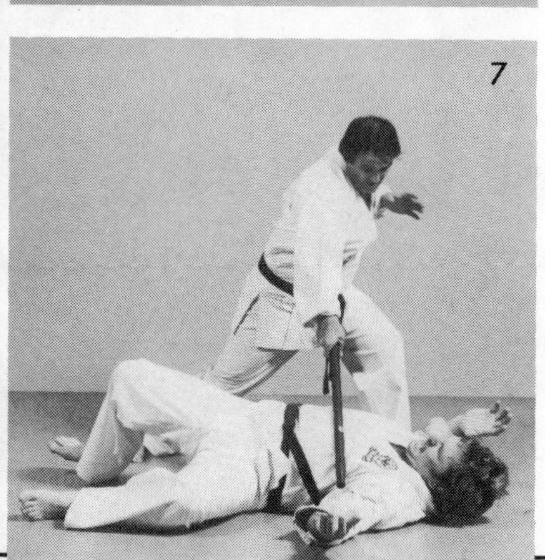
7

POKE AND STRIKE DEFENSE (Against Front Choke)

(1) As your attacker prepares to choke you, in one quick motion (2) lower your body weight by bending your knees slightly and thrust your

stick into his midsection. Then to prevent a further attack (3&4) strike a blow to the side of the knee.

LIFT AND PUSH DEFENSE (Against Front Choke)

This technique is particularly effective at breaking a choke hold against a larger person. As your opponent tries to choke you (1), take a quick breath of air and drop your weight. With a swift upward motion (2) use your body weight to de-

liver a blow to his elbows. Once you have driven the night stick upward (3), withdraw it very quickly (4) and use your weight to upset the attacker's balance by (5) driving the stick across his chest up to his armpits.

STEP AND STRIKE DEFENSE (Against Rear Choke)

(1) To break a rear choke, step forward (2) and pivot, drawing the stick ready to strike. Immediately deliver a snap strike to the groin (3&4), keeping a good grasp of the stick and preparing to move away after striking. If the attacker is still standing (5-8), a strike to the ribs should knock the wind out of him and make him lose his balance.

2

4

5

7

8

STEP AND LIFT DEFENSE (Against Rear Choke)

This technique enables you to control your attacker by using his own body weight to take him down. From a rear choke (1), take a quick breath and bend forward quickly (2), upsetting his balance. Step back behind his forward leg and pass

the night stick (3&4) behind his ankle with one hand and reach over and grasp the other end of the stick with your free hand. With a quick motion (5) pull upward with both hands, tripping him and maintaining a firm grasp on his foot.

POKE AND STRIKE DEFENSE
(Against Wrist Grab)

(1) When someone grabs your wrist, grasp the stick firmly in both hands and step sideways, leaning down on the stick (2) to throw him off balance. With your shoulders lowered, drive the stick (3) quickly at his solar plexus or rib cage, with the rear hand acting like a plunger. Follow through (4-7) with a groin strike to prevent further assault.

2

4

5

7

1

2

FRONT KICK DEFENSE (Against Stick Grab)

If an attacker grabs the front end of your night stick (1-3) and starts to pull it out of your hand, relax and let him think he has gained control over it. Don't let him up-

3

set your balance. With most of your weight on your back foot (4), use your front foot to kick his hand (5) holding the stick. Pull the stick away.

4

5

1

PUSH AND STRIKE DEFENSE
(Against Stick Grab)

When someone reaches out and grabs the very end of the night stick (1), don't try to meet force with force. Push the stick in the direction he is pulling it (2) with your hand closest to his. As he pulls, step in with a quick forward motion (3&4) and deliver a sharp blow to the solar plexus. Another strike (5&6) to the chin or chest area should loosen his grip completely. Try to use your hips to deliver power to your strike, and force your attacker backward off balance. If your opponent still does not let go (7-9), strike him on the side of the neck or on the clavicle.

4

7

2

3

5

6

8

9

WRIST TRAP DEFENSE
(Against Stick Grab)

(1&2) When an attacker grabs the end of your stick, move your hand closest to his and cover his fingers with your palm. Raise the front end of the stick upward quickly (3), rolling your wrist inward and bending his arm awkwardly and forcing his shoulder back. Drop your weight forward and to the right (4), loosening his grip. Seize his wrist securely (5) and pull the stick free (6). Strike him (7-9) in the knee or groin area.

2

3

5

6

8

9

1

4

WRIST TURN AND STRIKE DEFENSE
(Against Stick Grab)

The wrist turn is a variation on the wrist trap. The difference is, you do not grasp the attacker's fingers with your hand. Instead, you move your hand next to his grabbing hand (1&2) and turn the stick in a clockwise motion toward him (3) as you lift. Drop your weight quickly (4&5) and pull the night stick from his grasp. Snap him (6&7) on the wrist or hand. From this position, he may still be able to kick you or sweep your feet, so a blow (8-12) to the side of the kneecap may be necessary.

7

10

2
3
5
6
8
9
11
12

1

ELBOW LOCK AND STRIKE DEFENSE (Against Stick Grab)

A quick alternate technique when your attacker grabs one end of your stick (1&2) is to pull the front end downward slightly (3), making him react by trying to pull the stick toward him. Step in quickly (4) and lock your right elbow behind his right arm just above the elbow, thrusting hard (5) and pulling the stick down. He may let go at this point. Maintaining constant pressure, deliver a quick strike (6&7) against the back of his leg. Be especially careful; your gun side is exposed, and if you are not fast enough, your opponent is in a position to grab your weapon.

3

6

2
U.S.A.G.A.

4
U.S.A.G.A.

5
U.S.A.G.A.

7
U.S.A.G.A.

1

2

3

LIFT AND KICK DEFENSE (Against Two-Hand Stick Grab)

If your attacker grabs the stick with both hands (1&2) with his hands inside yours on the stick, the quickest method of control is to raise your arms quickly (3&4). Extending his arms upward, deliver a swift kick (5&6)

4

5

to the groin or kneecap. If he is concentrating on gaining control of the stick, he will not be prepared for a kick. Be aware that he may also try to kick you. If so, use your knees to block his kick.

6

CROSSOVER THROW DEFENSE
(Against Two-Hand Stick Grab)

Most people will try and grab your stick with both hands (1&2). When this happens, step in with your right foot (3-6) and use your right hand to force inward toward his right side. This should force him to turn toward his right shoulder. Try to twist his arms, keeping close body contact. Turning counter-clockwise, (7&8), trip him backward off his feet. You are now in a position (9-11) to deliver a blow to his midsection and immobilize him.

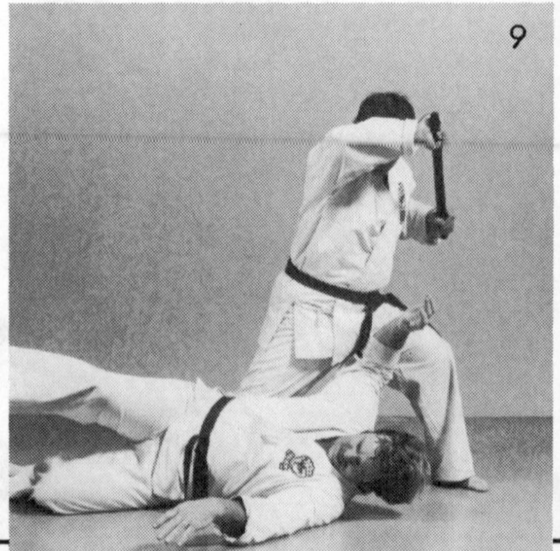

2

3

6

7

10

11

UNARMED DEFENSE

This section shows some ways to avoid being struck by someone who has a weapon when you do not, or if they have managed to take your night stick away from you.

1

2

DEFENSE AGAINST OVERHEAD ATTACK I

(1) When an attacker attempts to strike you with a weapon, or your own night stick which he has taken away from you, jump to one side to avoid the full power of the

blow (2), pivot into a wide forward stance and block his arm with your left hand (3), palm open. Reach over (4) and grasp his wrist in both hands and pull (5) his body forward using the

3

4

5

Continued on next page

Continued from preceding page

attacker's own momentum. With a quick snap motion (6) pull his arm backward and upward toward your left shoulder, keeping constant pressure on the wrist and forcing his stick hand

down toward the ground. When he releases the stick, force his head and shoulders (7&8) into the ground and (9&10) snap a strong strike to his midsection.

1

DEFENSE AGAINST OVERHEAD ATTACK II

When your attacker moves in with an overhand strike (1&2) and you are close enough, move in and under his strike. If your attacker has the stick in his right hand, step in with your right foot and wrap your arms (3) around his neck and the arm holding the stick, clasping your hands together. Step forward with your right foot, move your hip into his body (4) and lift quickly. Make sure your head is on the left side and that you drive your upper arm under his armpit, preventing him from using the night stick on you. Once you have gained control of the attacker on the ground (5&6), strike him (7&8) on the knee or midsection.

3

6

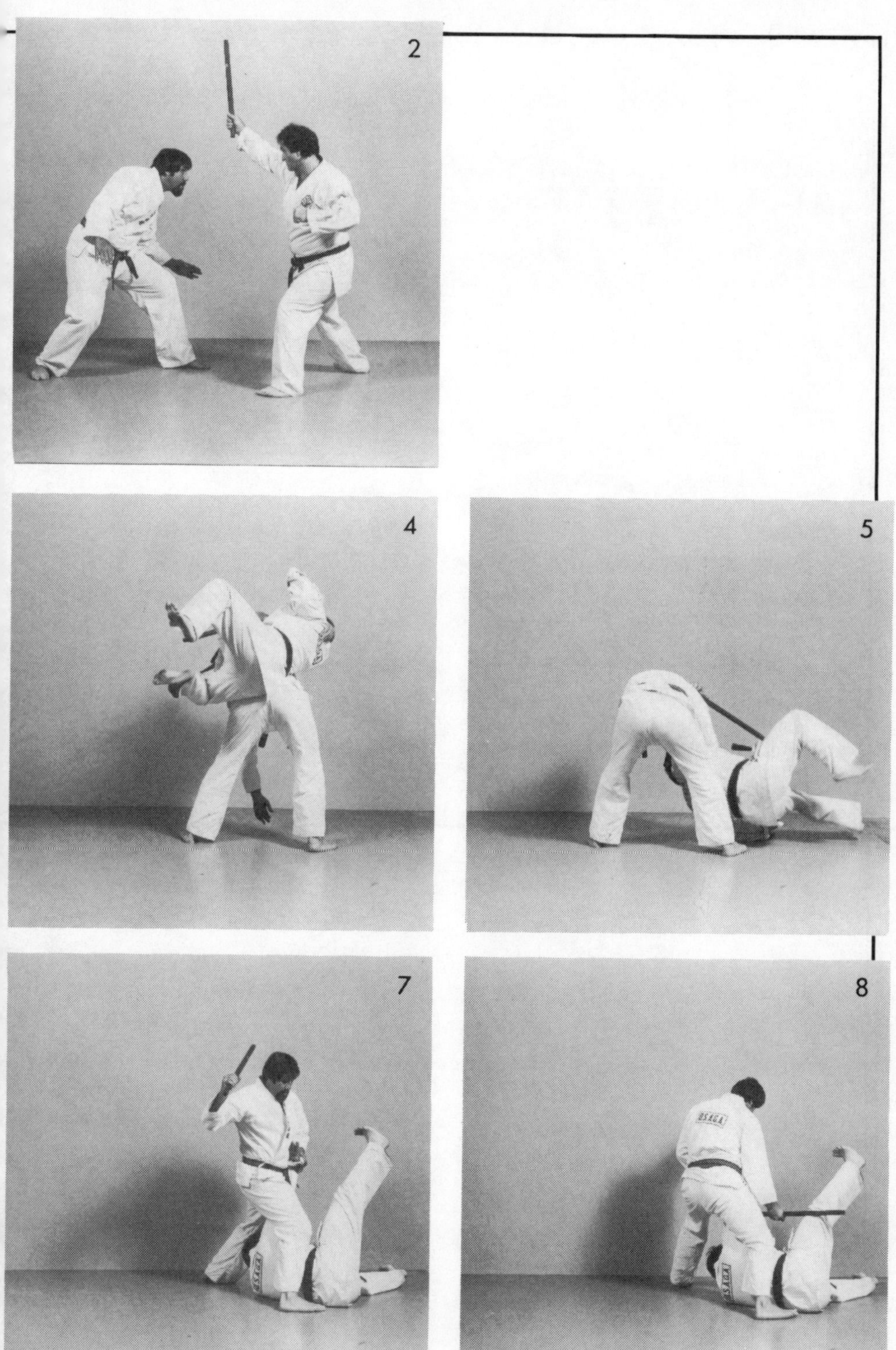
2
4
5
7
8

DEFENSE AGAINST OVERHEAD ATTACK III

(1) If your attacker comes at you with a raised right-hand strike to the head, step in quickly with your right foot (2&3) and grab his wrist with your right hand. Spin to the left (4) while pulling on his wrist and execute an elbow smash (5) in the face or neck. Follow up immediately (6&7) with a hammer-fist or open-hand strike to the groin.

2

4

5

7

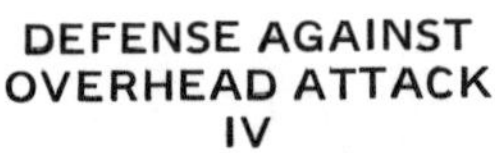

DEFENSE AGAINST OVERHEAD ATTACK IV

(1) When an attacker prepares for an overhead strike, step in close (2&3) and block his wrist with your right hand. When you contact the wrist, place your left arm over his striking hand (4) and pull your right hand

inward and his wrist against your chest. (5) Use an elbow smash to the face or a quick turning motion to your right (6) so that you may strike him in the side of the neck.

DEFENSE AGAINST OVERHEAD ATTACK V

Using a two-hand grab to grasp the attacker's wrist before he can strike (1-3), twist to your right and use your left arm to come down on his right arm (4-6), forcing him with his own momentum to the ground. You are now in a position to grab the stick (7) from him. Use a wrist submission by twisting his right hand counterclockwise and (8-10) striking him on the shoulder.

2
3
5
6
9
10

Arrest Techniques: Come-along Holds and Choke Holds

At times it becomes necessary to compel a suspect to move where you want him to when he resists. These moves must be practiced regularly to avoid improper application of the stick which could cause serious injury. Study the techniques carefully, especially the choke holds. Applying a choke hold incorrectly can lead to accidental death. Even when properly applying the hold, it should only be held a few minutes at best and only in extreme cases of resistance.

ARM LIFT I

This hold can be applied for short distances. Clasp your hands with the suspect (1&2) and jerk down to straighten his arm (3) and throw him off balance. With the stick in your left hand, extend it under his arm and over his right shoulder (4), placing the stick against his neck near the base of the skull. The

end of the stick presses just below the ear. Turn his palm upward away from his body (5) and press the stick upward against the elbow nerve of his outstretched arm. Continue twisting his right hand down and away, applying pressure (6) to the base of his neck and the back of his elbow.

ARMPIT HOLD

This is an excellent maneuver for controlling someone who is trying to pull away from you. Reach out (1&2) and grasp his right hand. Turn his wrist counterclockwise and place the night stick (3&4) under his armpit and into the

3

nerve center located directly under his shoulder. Twisting his arm and keeping constant pressure on the underside of his arm, you should be able to walk him for a short distance with no problem.

BAR HAMMERLOCK

To force a suspect to come along (1), place the night stick in your right hand and run it alongside the inside portion of his right arm (2) touching the wrist. Let your thumb stick out to act as a stopper. With your thumb around his wrist, push his arm back (3) and raise the wrist, palm upward. Using your left hand on the stick, push his shoulder downward (4&5), making sure to keep a tight grip on the wrist in your right hand. Place your left arm across the bend of his elbow (6) and remove the stick (7), placing it (8) across his chest. Apply pressure with the left hand on his elbow and (9) lift him up. Make sure you do not press against his throat.

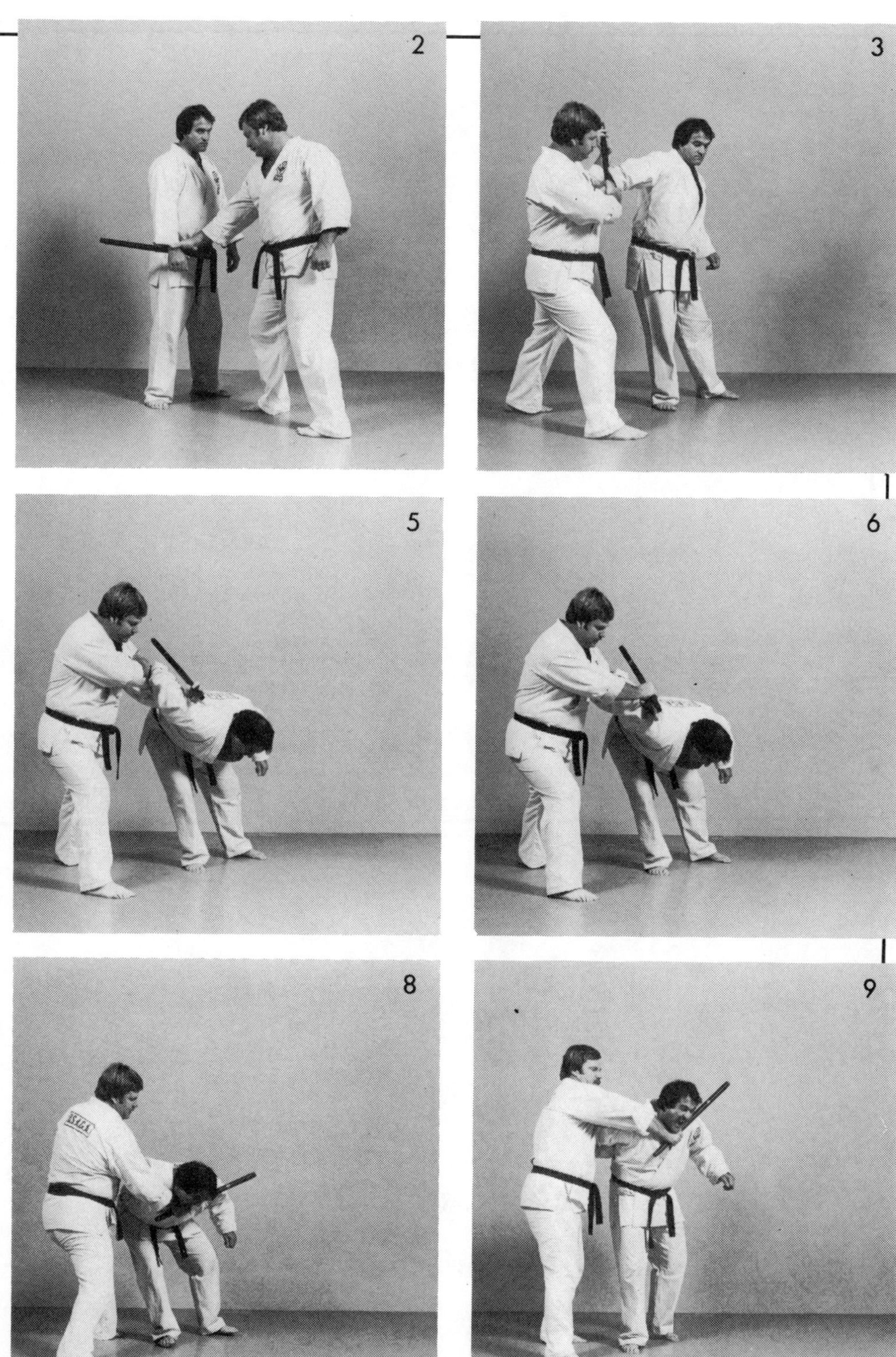
2
3
5
6
8
9

1

2

ARM LIFT II

To walk a suspect forward, grasp his right wrist (1-3), placing your night stick across your chest with the front end on your right shoulder. Pull his arm across the front of your body toward your right shoulder, raising his arm at the same time. Step in with your left foot and place the night stick directly under his elbow (4) as you pivot. Use an upward pushing motion with your left hand and a downward pulling motion with your right hand. You can add extra pressure if necessary on his rib cage by placing your left elbow against his body. If your attacker should try and get away, a quick push forward on his elbow will force him to the ground.

1

2

GROIN LIFT

For this come-along technique, grasp the night stick in the middle with your right hand and place your left hand (1&2) on the suspect's left shoulder. Slip the stick quickly through his legs (3) and lock the stick against the front of

his thighs. Lift up with pressure on his groin, using your free hand on his shoulder (4&5) to move him forward. Make sure that your palm faces upward, making it hard for him to push the stick out of your hand.

ARM LOCK

(1) When approaching a suspect from the rear, place the night stick in your right hand just under your armpit, letting about 15 inches of the stick protrude forward. Be cautious of the suspect turning quickly or trying a back kick. Grab his left wrist with your free (left) hand (2) and place the stick under his armpit (3), getting in close to his body with the stick still under your armpit. Begin to lift his

wrist up (4) and place the night stick across the top of his wrist with your left hand. Switch your grip to your fingers and apply pressure to the wrist with the top of the stick. Reach underneath his wrist with your right hand (5&6) and grab the end of the stick, pulling down with your right hand and raising your right elbow. The stick is now locked across the nerve endings of his wrist.

1

2

SHOULDER LIFT

(1) When your suspect is kneeling on the ground and refuses to get up, place the night stick under his left armpit (2), across his shoulder and up behind his neck (3&4). With a steady pushing motion on the front end of the stick (using the left hand) and a steady lifting motion with the butt end, try to force him to stand. If he tries to pull you off balance, apply quick pressure to the front end of the stick and force him down again.

3

4

CHOKE HOLDS

The crossed-arm or rear V choke hold is quite effective for short distances. It may be applied to an individual who refuses to move from an area (such as a demonstration or sit-in).

1

REAR V CHOKE HOLD

The night stick is held in the right hand (1&2) with the palm facing toward the ground, placed on the person's left shoulder. By placing the stick in front of him you have a better pulling motion should he try to lean forward and pull you off guard. Apply a slight pressure against the side of the neck with the outside portion of your wrist, pulling the stick inward toward the side of his neck. Reach over with your right arm (3) and grasp the night stick near the end. You have now formed a V block, which should stop any sudden movement. To maintain a constant pressure without stopping his intake of air, bring both of your hands as snug as possible against the sides of his neck with a slight upward motion of your elbows. Make sure that your palms face the ground and that you do not keep this hold on too long or you may cause severe injury.

2

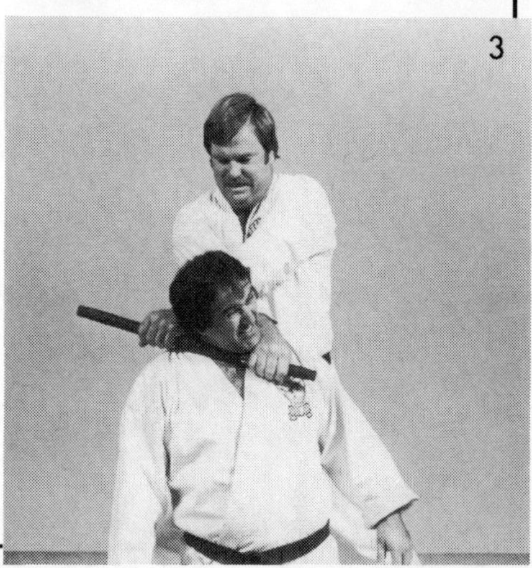
3

This type of choke hold is only used in extreme cases of resistance, particularly if the suspect is high on drugs. The hold must be applied very carefully and not too long. *If you apply too*

REAR LOCK STRANGLEHOLD

The stick is held in the right hand (1&2) and placed across the chest (3) facing up at a 45-degree angle. After you have applied upward pressure with your right hand, reach down and place your left hand (4) under the night stick. The top end of the stick

much pressure you can cause severe damage or even death. If the suspect is high on drugs, he may not experience the pain and you might apply too much force.

should be resting on your left shoulder. To complete this hold, reach up (5&6) and place your left hand behind the suspect's head. Make sure that the stick is placed on the side of the neck and not on the Adam's apple.

Car-in/Car-out Techniques

The following techniques are designed for removing an uncooperative suspect from a vehicle or to compel a suspect into your patrol car—both common instances of resistance when a police officer encounters opposition.

These are aggressive techniques, so if you decide to use them you have obviously made the decision that only force will accomplish your immediate objective (that is, an arrest). If you are not skilled in these moves, however, your chances of injuring the suspect are greater—making your arrest that much more complicated. Follow the instructions given here carefully and devote a lot of practice to them.

1

2

CAR-IN/WRIST SMASH AND GROIN LIFT

When a suspect uses the top of the car or door to resist (1), use the night stick to hit and press down on his forearm or wrist (2), feeding his arm down through his groin area (3). This ties up the use of his hand and upsets his balance. Reach under with your left hand and grab the night stick, lifting upward (4) and keeping the night stick across his trapped wrist. Reach up with the right hand (5) and force him down into the car, grasping his clothing in the center of his back. After he is in the vehicle, be especially careful he does not kick you while lying on the seat.

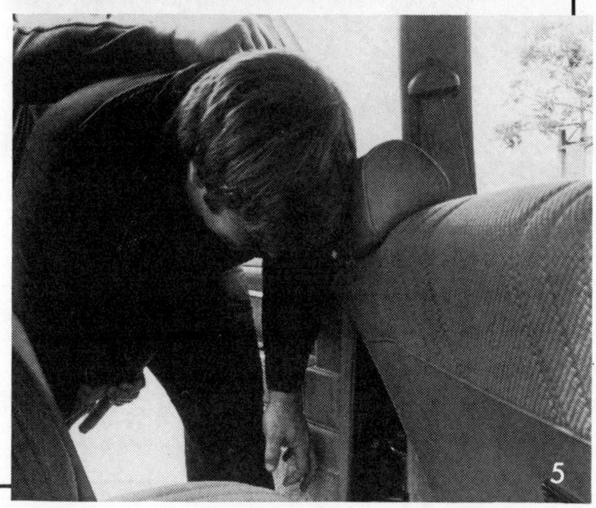

1

2

CAR-IN/NECK DROP

(1) If the suspect places both hands on the top of the car, slide the stick under his right arm (2), grab his wrist and lift (3) as you press down on the back of his neck with the stick. The stick should

3

also be pressing (4) on his elbow. Continue applying pressure to the neck and elbow while grasping the wrist (5). This forward motion should force him into the car.

4

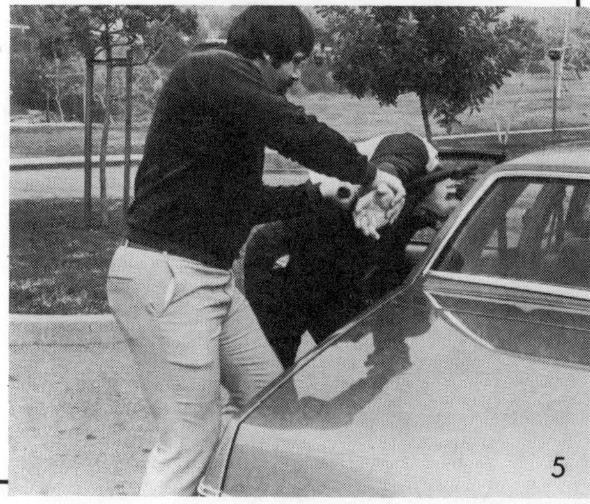
5

1

2

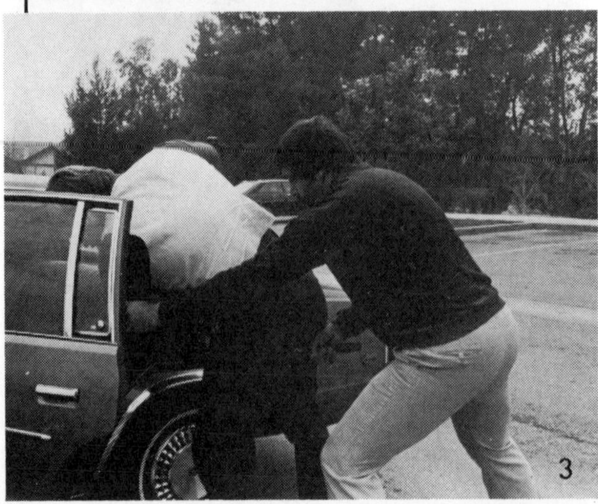

3

CAR-IN/GROIN LIFT

When a suspect is resisting attempts to place him in the car, the groin lift can be used. Place the night stick in your right hand and feed it through his legs (1) quickly, holding the stick near the end and close to his body. Reach around with your left hand (2) grab the front end of the night stick and lift up with a quick motion with both hands. Use your right hand to force him forward. When he is off balance, reach up with the left hand and grab his shoulder (3), pushing him down into the car as you continue lifting with the right hand and stick. Be especially careful that he does not strike his head on the top of the vehicle.

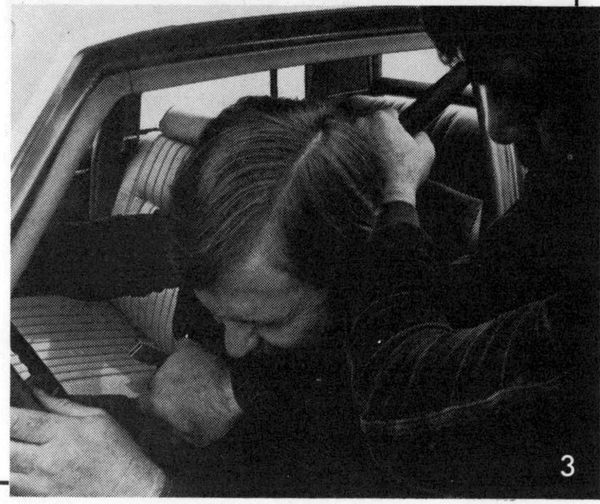

CAR-OUT/CROSSOVER CHOKE HOLD

Keep your body close to the car. With the night stick in your right hand, palm down (1), place the stick across the opposite side of the driver's neck with your arm touching the neck as well. Reach in with your left hand (2) and grab the front end of the stick behind his head. Your arms now form a V-shape. In this lock he will not be able to break the hold. Pull your right hand down toward the ground (3) while your left hand behind his neck pulls toward you. This will pry him out of the vehicle. (Do **not** apply too much pressure around the neck.)

CAR-OUT/PRY AND WEDGE

For this move (1), place the night stick against the back of his elbow and into his groin area. Grab his left wrist (2&3) and pull up while exerting pressure on the back

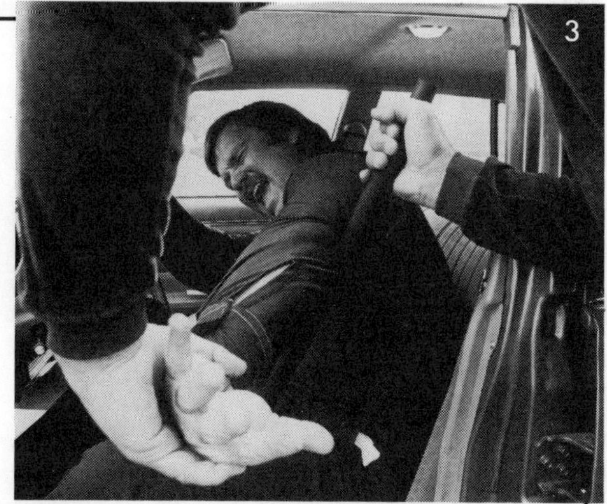

of his elbow. Make sure you have a strong finger hold, twisting his wrist counterclockwise (4) and keeping pressure on his arm. (5) This will force him out of the car.

1

2

3

CAR-OUT/ARM LIFT

(1) When a suspect refuses to get out of his car, reach in and grab his left arm with your left hand (2) while at the same time placing the night stick under his left armpit and pushing it against the side of his neck. Forcing his body forward against the steer-

ing wheel (3), pull him out of the car (4-6) by applying constant pressure on the back of his neck and against the elbow nerve while pulling back up and on the wrist. Do not let your stick slip from behind his neck.

CAR-OUT/SIDE NECK CHOKE HOLD

(1) When your suspect refuses to come out, place the night stick on the right side of his neck, holding the stick in the left hand (2) and using your right hand to reach behind him and grab (3) the front end of the stick. Pull upward with the right hand (4&5)

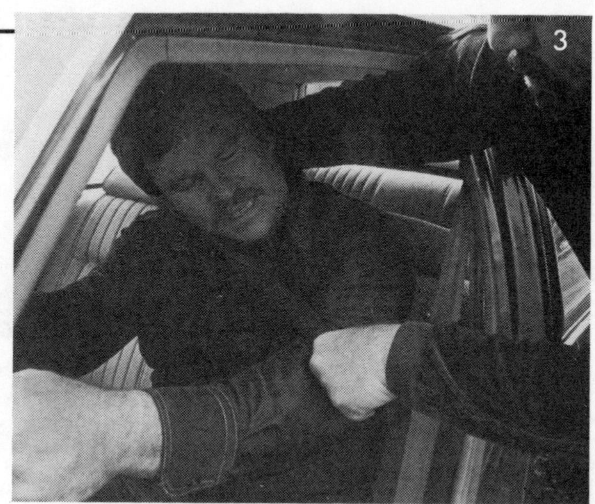

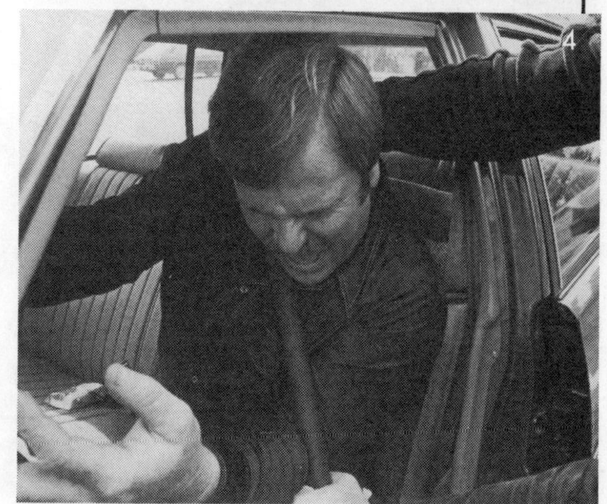

against the side of his neck and your left hand toward his left shoulder. **Do not apply too much pressure.** Once he is out of the car, use a come-along hold. Note: Your left hand pushes continually against his left arm, making it hard for him to try a counterstrike.

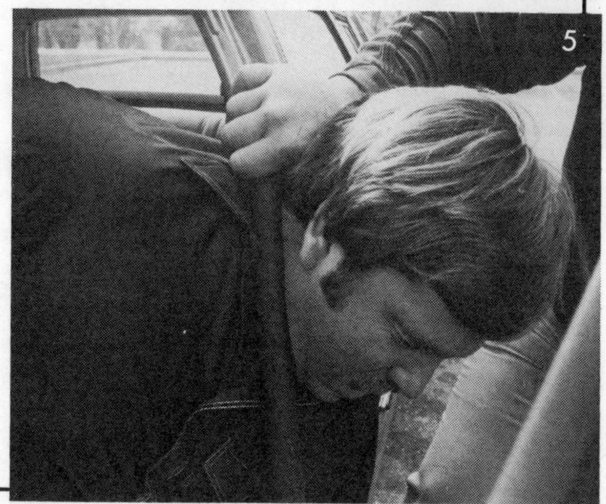

CAR-OUT/ARMPIT LIFT

(1&2) When a suspect refuses to get out of his car, reach across with your left hand and grab him on his left wrist. Push the night stick against the back of his left arm (3&4) and under his armpit. The stick should be poking into the nerve of his armpit. Twist his thumb clockwise (5&6). If he should start to slip away from you, keep a steady grasp on his thumb and strike him across the lower ribs. Raise him up (7-9) and out of the car, placing his arm against the car and using a prying motion if necessary.

1

4

7

2

3

5

6

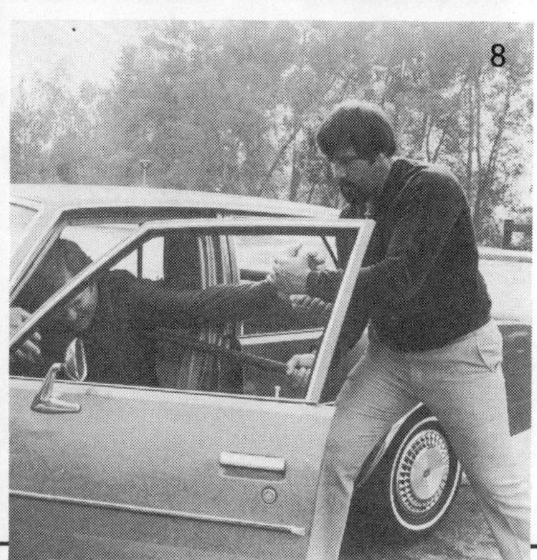
8

9

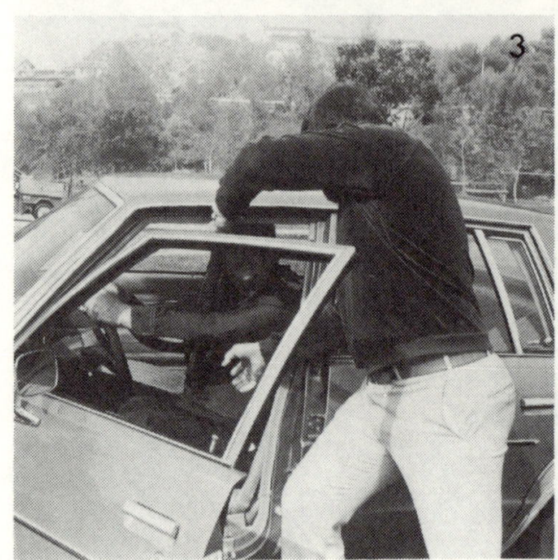

CAR-OUT/BAR HAMMERLOCK

This technique is particulary useful if the person appears to be stronger than you. Reach over with the night stick (1-3) in your left hand and place it across the inside of his upper arm (bicep). Feed it through, grasping the front end of the stick with your right hand and pushing downward quickly on his wrist with your left hand. Twist the stick (4-7) by pulling down with your left hand and pushing up with your right hand. Try to force his wrist back up toward the small of his back, and push against his shoulder with your right hand. Force him past the door opening and to the ground.

2

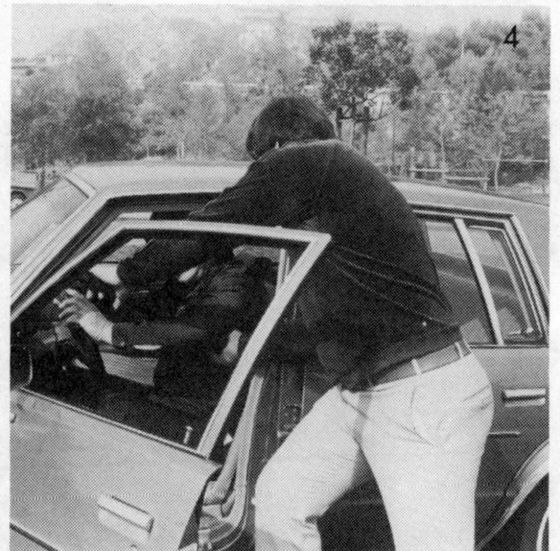
4

5

7

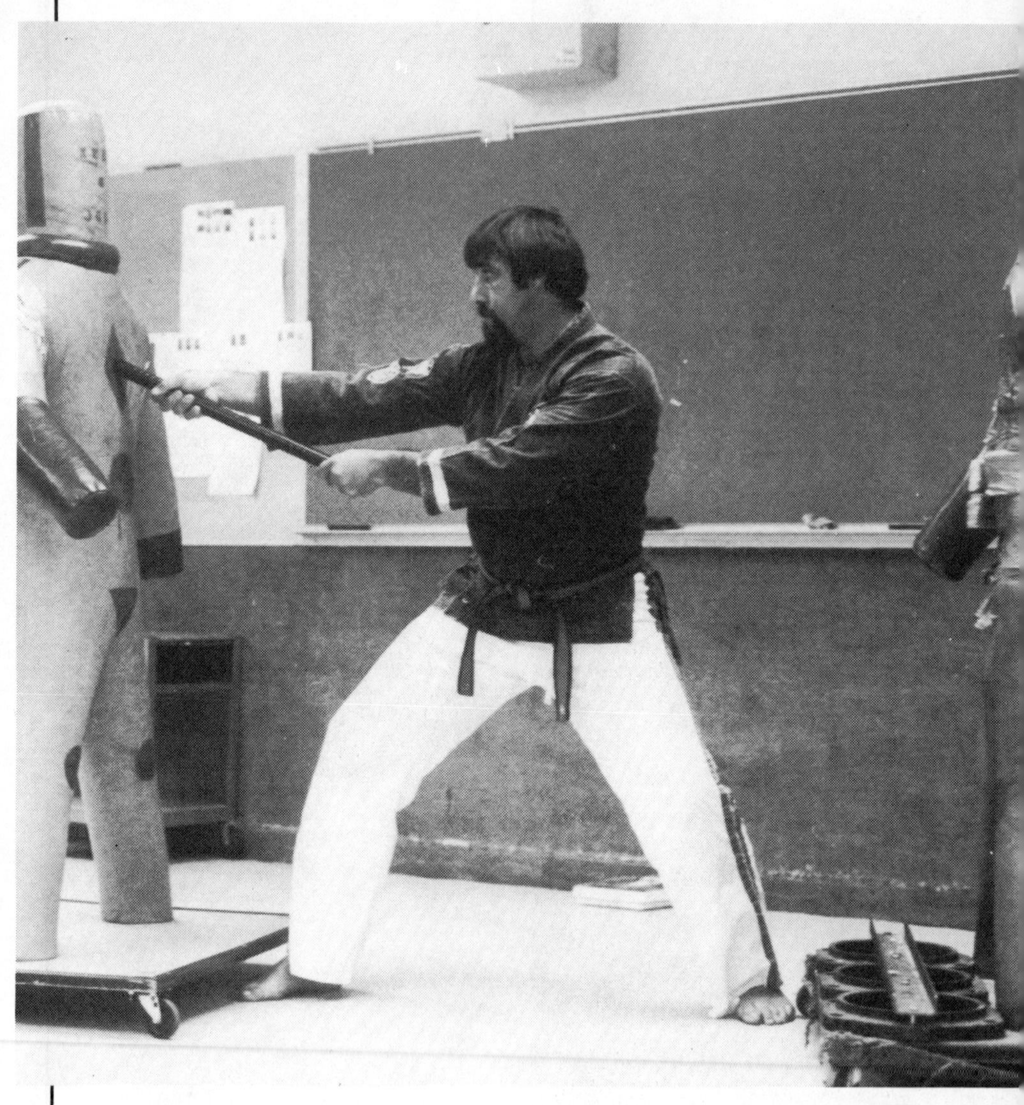

Special Exercises and Striking Drills

This chapter illustrates exercises and special drills for one or two people that are used to help maintain proper coordination and skill with the night stick. Becoming proficient with the night stick means regular practice and constant application of the proper stances, blocks, snap strikes and draws already covered in this book. The first section concentrates on drills using the legs and arms. The second section shows practice in striking areas of the body using a dummy.

SNAP AND CATCH DRILL

Note: Use only a practice rubber night stick for this and the following drills.

The object of this exercise is to establish speed and coordination with the wrist and upper arm. Face your partner, assuming a wide stance (1), holding the stick palm down. Try to snap the stick quickly (2&3) with a strike to the stomach, just above the

3

belt. The speed strike should be fast enough to snap the midsection and bring the stick back to its original position without your partner grabbing it (4). If he is able to grab it, your wrist is too tight. You must be flexible enough to snap it and recover the stick for an effective strike. Repeat this exercise with the other hand.

4

1

2

3

BLOCK AND STRIKE DRILL

The object of this drill is to have your partner try to reach out and grab your shoulder with either hand (without telling you which one he will use). You must react in one fluid motion (1-3), blocking his wrist with a snap motion and then

4

5

immediately delivering a low deflection strike (4-6) to his leg area. You can add speed to this exercise if you have your partner try to reach down and grab the stick from you when you deliver the strike.

6

FRONT EXCHANGE DRILL

This drill is for timing and dexterity. (1) Beginning with the stick in a ready position, bring the stick up with the right hand (2) and pass it up and over your right shoulder (3), grabbing it with your left hand (4). Bring the stick across the front of your body (5) and repeat the same motion (6-8) with your left hand. Start out slow and build up speed as you continue the left-right exchange for about a minute. Try to keep the motions fluid, concentrating on your hand grip each time you catch the stick.

2
4
5
7
8

REAR EXCHANGE DRILL

The rear exchange drill (1-7) begins just like the front exchange, only here you reach across the back instead of the front of your body to make the catch. This exercise could also be alternated with the front exchange drill. You might also do this drill while taking a step forward and then backward, practicing balance. Do this drill for about one minute, picking up speed as you switch the stick from hand to hand.

2
U.S.A.G.A.

4
U.S.A.G.A.

5
U.S.A.G.A.

7
U.S.A.G.A.

1

2

3

LEG FEED DRILL

This is a good exercise for timing and coordination. Holding the night stick in the right hand (1), lift your left leg off the ground (2) and pass the stick underneath (3), grabbing it with your left hand. Repeat the procedure in the opposite direction (4-6), feeding the stick under the right leg and grabbing it with your right hand. Do this exercise for at least one minute, trying to pick up speed as you go. When your balance and timing are really improved, try this drill with your eyes closed.

4

5

6

1

2

3

THROWING AND RECEIVING

This drill will build up your reflexes, and help you develop better eye-to-eye contact on moving targets. A situation often develops where someone will toss you a stick or throw you one that has been dropped. Face your partner (1) while holding your night stick in your right hand. Simultaneously, toss your sticks (2&3) to each other. The object is to keep the sticks moving as fast as you both can throw them, without dropping either stick.

TARGET THROWING DRILL

In most cases it is extremely inadvisable to throw your stick at an attacker. He might turn right around and use it against you. However, you may find that it becomes necessary to trip up an attacker, especially if he is armed. Drop your weight and set in a well-balanced stance (1) with a firm grip on your night stick. With a steady motion, snap your wrist (2-4) and follow through by extending your throwing arm in the direction of the target. Practicing this drill will improve your accuracy. Note: Do **not** practice this drill using a real person as a target.

These drills should be practiced on a striking dummy, not a real person. The butt strike (1) is delivered to the side of the neck. If you are delivering the blow with the left hand, step in with the left leg for more power. Strike the dummy and snap back into the ready position. Repeat this quickly at least 15 times. Repeat the drill using the right leg and right hand.

(2) The push strike. Lean in with the right foot and strike the dummy high in the chest, delivering the maximum amount of power. Alternate. Repeat this 15 times.

APPLICATION

APPLICATION

(3) When striking the upper-chest area, deliver the forward blow with a slight upward motion, into the solar plexus. Your stance should be wide and balanced. Lock the arms out in position each time you strike. Repeat.

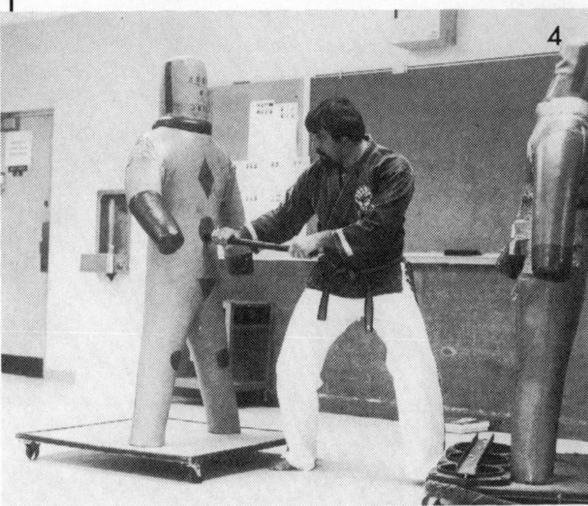

(4) The body weight should be forward and the stance narrower for a strike to the midsection. The palms may be either up or down. Repeat.

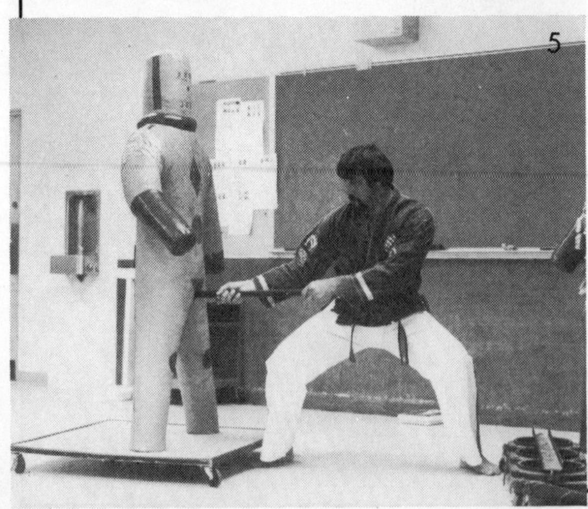

(5) When delivering a groin strike, drop your weight low, keeping the shoulders on an even plane. Strike hard and fast. Repeat.

APPLICATION

APPLICATION

APPLICATION

(6) The side poke is quite effective in close areas where your range is limited. Hold the stick near the middle, and turn your body into the strike for maximum power. The leading foot should be the same as the hand leading the strike. Try delivering the strike with both hands, one hand grasping the stick firmly at each end.

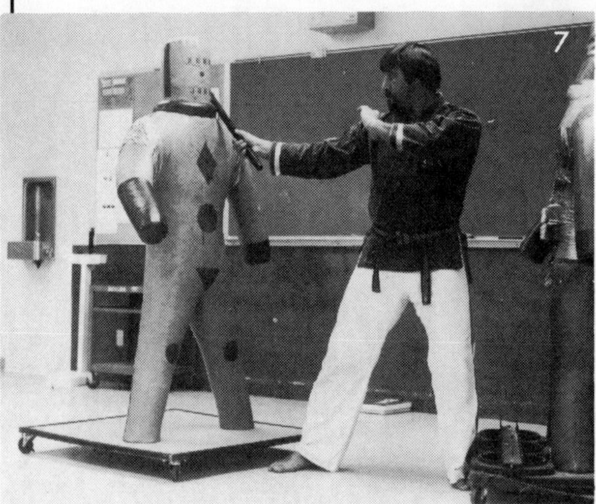

(7) A strike near the side of the neck should be delivered with a lot of snap. Try to snap the arm fully extended so you can obtain maximum striking distance, out of the attacker's reach. Repeat this drill 15 times on either side of the neck.

(8) For strikes when you are being approached from the rear. Swivel with your shoulders and hips, right or left, and let your arm snap into the strike, watching your attacker over your shoulder. Repeat this drill by alternating from left to right, quickly.

APPLICATION

APPLICATION

APPLICATION

(9) Groin strike. When your attacker approaches from behind, snap as you step forward away from your attacker. Repeat this drill 25 times on each side, alternating right and left.

(10) Use the same steps as in the groin strike, but snap to the legs, especially the knees. Hold the stick near the butt end to give you the farthest striking distance between you and your attacker. Step forward away from the attacker with either leg, then alternate.

(11) With this variation of the rear strike, you deliver the blow to the midsection, holding the stick near the center and stepping away to leave room between you and your opponent.

I

APPLICATION

J

APPLICATION

K

APPLICATION